WOMEN OF WORTH
Jewish Women in Britain

Exhibition at Manchester Jewish Museum
24th May 1992 - January 1993

Research and text: Frances Guy

Research and editorial advisors: Rickie Burman and Bill Williams

Introduction

Jewish women have been neglected by historians, both as women and as members of a minority community. Now the experiences of Jewish women are being recorded as part of the wider process of recovering the heritage of those who have previously lacked a voice in history.

'Women of Worth' does not present a definitive account of Jewish women's history in Britain, but highlights the variety of roles that Jewish women have undertaken in the past and their differing experiences in the present day. It focuses on the lives of 'ordinary' Jewish women and also recognises the contribution of some individual women who have had a substantial impact on the Jewish community.

'Women of Worth' looks beyond the stereotype of the Jewish mother and the Jewish 'princess', the traditional ways in which Jewish women have been portrayed by others. The exhibition presents alternative images of Jewish women which are based on fact rather than fantasy.

The booklet is in four sections. This first section provides an introduction to the subject of Jewish women's history and looks at the ways in which Jewish women have been represented by others.

The second section, 'History', describes the position of the established Jewish community in Victorian Britain. It examines the impact that the arrival of immigrant Jews from Eastern Europe in the late 19th century had on the women in Anglo-Jewry.

The third section, 'Themes', outlines the major roles and concerns of Jewish women in both the established and the immigrant communities between the years 1850 and 1945. It covers women's involvement in areas such as work and politics, and highlights the changes that were taking place in the position of women in society during this period.

The final section, 'Developments', is a brief summary of Jewish women's history in more recent years, a time of confrontation and change for many women. The section ends with the thoughts of some Jewish women as they reflect on their role in the community today.

REPRESENTATIONS OF JEWISH WOMEN

In the 19th century, Jewish women were portrayed according to a complex code of representation which was based on the anti-Semitism of British society and Victorian notions of sexuality and morality.

In political propaganda and in other visual and literary media, portrayals of Jewish women, like those of non-Jewish women, at once embodied the polarities of 'virgin' and 'whore'. Such images were intensified by society's associations of middle-class Jews with wealth and ostentation, and a general belief that immigrant Jews were harbingers of disease and moral depravity.

In addition, women of Sephardi origin were subject to the Western fantasy of the 'Orient', a way of thinking that depicted the countries of the Middle East as places of exoticism and sensuality. The repressed sexuality of Victorian Britain found an outlet in representations of these 'Oriental' women, who were seen to exist outside the narrow constraints of Western society.

Jewish women were also stereotyped by their own community, the image of the Jewish mother being the most powerful example. Over the years, the resilient woman of the 'shtetl' became the 'Yiddishe Mama', the butt of many Jewish jokes. This caricature was taken up by the wider society where the Jewish mother became an object of ridicule and scorn, a pervasive and damaging misrepresentation which is still very much alive today.

'The Sephardic Jewish type... pathetically noble and beautiful in a woman, so suggestive of chastity and the most passionate love combined - love conjugal and filial and maternal - love that implies all the big practical obligations and responsibilities of human life, that the mere term "Jewess"... brings to my mind some vague, mysterious, exotically poetic image of all I love best in women.'
George du Maurier in 'The Martian', 1897.

'Mrs. Levine, her face wreathed in proud smiles, was pushing her baby-carriage along Wilshire Boulevard in Los Angeles, taking her infant daughter on her first outing. On the way she encountered a neighbour who gushed over the baby.
"What a beautiful child!" the neighbour cried.
Mrs. Levine smiled delightedly. "This is nothing," she boasted. "You should see her pictures!"'

History

JEWISH VICTORIANS

The history of the Jewish community in Britain reads as a continuous struggle against prejudice and for the right to be recognised as equal members of British society.

During the Victorian era, it looked as if the struggle was about to come to an end.

Anglo-Jewry was developing into a largely middle-class community, living in the better districts of London and the provincial towns, and was integrating successfully into English cultural and economic life. In 1858, the Anglo-Jewish community finally achieved political equality in Britain when Baron Lionel de Rothschild became the first Jew to be admitted into the House of Commons.

However, this new-found acceptance was put in danger later in the 19th century. Large numbers of Jewish immigrants began to flee to Britain from Eastern Europe, where poverty and anti-Semitic persecution had reached new levels. They settled in the industrial centres of Britain, where accommodation was cheapest and work, although unskilled and poorly paid, was relatively plentiful. Within the new immigrant community many of the customs of the 'shtetl', the typical Jewish settlement of Eastern Europe, survived.

The Anglo-Jewish community, which had adopted

2

the values of the Victorian upper and middle classes, felt that its position was threatened by the influx of working-class immigrants and their 'foreign' ways. These fears proved well-founded as sections of British society protested at the arrival of what they saw as 'alien invaders'. Anti-Semitism increased and the Government prepared immigration laws in an effort to stop the flow of foreigners into Britain.

The established Anglo-Jewish community reacted by taking on the responsibility for the immigrants' welfare. Motivated both by Jewish traditions of charity and by their own self-interest, the community founded many different organisations which, while offering much-needed support, also aimed to educate the immigrant population in Victorian values and to make them 'worthy' of British citizenship.

A WOMAN'S PLACE

The established Anglo-Jewish community upheld the Victorian ideal of separate roles for men and women. Before the end of the 19th century, such education as middle-class girls received emphasised lady-like accomplishments or practical domestic skills in preparation for life as a married woman. Most people expected women to stay in the home whilst their husbands went out to earn a living.

Even in the home, the activities of women were limited since most middle and upper class families employed servants to clean and cook for the household. Victorian society saw the woman as the spiritual guardian of her home, a role enhanced for

Jewish women by the domestic rituals expected of them in religious law.

The only acceptable public roles open to middle-class women were those of society hostess or charity worker. Such activities, despite projecting women into the male arena of public life, were seen by society to magnify women's spiritual and feminine qualities.

As models of femininity, women in the Anglo-Jewish community sought to encourage immigrant women to conform to Victorian moral standards and to adopt 'English' patterns of behaviour. Middle-class women were particularly active in communal schools, where they taught the appropriate domestic skills and instilled society's expectations in their female pupils.

Ironically, although Anglo-Jewish women were concerned to encourage immigrant women to remain in the home, the result of their charitable work gained them increasing acceptance in public life and a growing desire for change in their unequal position in religious and secular society.

'The future of our race will depend on the goodness of the women, and that while all cannot be clever and beautiful, each one can improve the world by cultivating gentleness, piety, firmness and graciousness.'
Miss Raphael, Headmistress of the Manchester Jews' School, speaking at a Conference of Jewish Women, 1902.

'Miss Raphael wasn't concerned with cleverness. She was more concerned with etiquette and being ladies and walking properly and table manners and you've got to behave yourself in the street.'

Annie A., speaking about the Headmistress of the Manchester Jews' School.

'Her duty is to make home happy; her mission, to influence man, alike in her relative duties of mother to her son, wife to her husband, sister to her brother, and, in her own person, to upraise the holy cause of religion... To obtain this superiority is to become more spiritual; for in that single word every feminine grace and Jewish requisite is comprised.'
Grace Aguilar, in 'The Women of Israel', 1845.

CHANGING TRADITIONS

An important focus in the established community's programme of anglicisation was the practice of religion in the immigrant population.

In Eastern Europe, the Jewish faith was at the heart of 'shtetl' life. Traditionally, it was acceptable for men to devote their time to the study of Hebrew and Judaism, and people saw religious scholarship as the route to respect and social prestige. The role of married women was to support their husbands in this pursuit of knowledge by taking paid work in addition to their household duties and by upholding Jewish customs in the home.

On their arrival in Britain, immigrant families encountered a more secular society in which material, not religious, success was the key to social status. Victorian society expected the man to be the main breadwinner of the family. Although married women in the immigrant population had, of necessity, to supplement the family income, the established Anglo-Jewish community exerted pressure upon them to give up work after marriage.

In addition to encouraging immigrant wives to relinquish their traditional role of supporting their husbands, Anglo-Jewry also discouraged them from what it saw as 'unbecoming' aspects of Jewish religious law, such as the wearing of 'sheitels' or wigs after marriage. However, the role of women in maintaining a 'kosher' home and carrying out domestic rituals remained largely the same, despite the secular nature of society.

Overleaf: Postcard of a woman kindling the Sabbath candles, c1918. Manchester Jewish Museum.
Preparing for the Sabbath was one of women's most important religious roles. This included cooking the meal according to Jewish dietary laws, making and blessing the Sabbath loaf or 'challah', and lighting the candles on a Friday evening.

4

Themes

THE WORKPLACE

In Victorian society, most people believed that a woman's place was in the home. The established Anglo-Jewish community upheld this ideal in order to be more readily accepted into the wider society. Those middle-class women who became teachers or nurses after school usually had to cease working and depend on their husbands for support once they were married.

However, immigrant women arrived from Eastern Europe with a strong tradition of work outside the home after marriage, and the struggle for economic survival in Britain ensured that this continued. It was only very gradually that pressure from the established community persuaded them to conform to Victorian expectations.

Most immigrant women found their way into the garment trade, chiefly in workshops owned by immigrant men. Married women also entered such occupations as market-trading and shopkeeping, and it was not unusual for a woman to have her own business. Increasingly, under the established community's pressure, married women carried out their paid work in the home. This included piece-work for the tailoring industry and taking in lodgers. In addition, women had responsibility for the household chores and economised to make the family's meagre income go further.

'My father was really, really no businessman to speak of at all... But mother was a sharp businesswoman. She did

all the business advising at that time, as far as I remember.'
Rachel B., Manchester.

'From the time that I recollect my mother, she'd always been going on the markets. She always told us, "Don't depend upon your husband's wage. Go out and earn your own."'
Sarah M., Manchester.

'My mother would get some bones, onion, a potato. She'd fry the onions, then put water and bones in with them, and then when that was well boiled up, put cornflour and flour in, thicken it, then put boiled potatoes in. That was the meal. I think it cost "flumpence", that. Again, we've all lived to a good age on it.'
Phil G., Manchester.

WAR AND WORK

The First World War brought new opportunities for women in the workplace. Jewish women in the established community found new roles for themselves in the British war effort and, like non-Jewish women, many volunteered their services as nurses.

Many men in the Anglo-Jewish community were eager to fight for their country in the First World War in order to prove their loyalty to Britain. As a result, women in the immigrant community found that the burden of providing for themselves and their families fell on their own shoulders, sometimes for the first time. Some women set up small businesses such as shops and laundries, while others stepped into jobs vacated by immigrant men who had gone off to fight. Elsewhere, women became acquainted with traditionally 'masculine' types of work in factories and engineering, although they had to accept lower rates of pay.

Once the war had ended, most of these women surrendered their new occupations as the male workforce returned. The pressure from the established community and the wider society for women to stay in the home became greater and the ideal of separate roles for men and women became a reality for most women.

However, Britain's economy was changing and the campaign for women's rights was gaining more recognition. With increased education and training, some Jewish women were able to enter new and 'respectable' occupations, especially in the expanding field of clerical work.

'In those days, not the rule but the custom was... a Jewish girl got married - it was her duty to stay at home and look after her home and husband... Those days, a man was king in his castle... It was a very rare thing for a Jewish girl to get married and go out to work.'
Minnie C., Manchester, speaking about those women who ceased to go out to work after marriage in the 1920s and 1930s.

'It wasn't done in those days. Before you got married, you left work two weeks before and I've never been back to work since. And I wish I could have done then, because I would have earned more than my husband earned, but you didn't do it, it was just not done, it wasn't the thing... you'd rather starve and not go.'
Pearl G., Manchester.

THE POLITICS OF THE WORKPLACE

Most women in the Anglo-Jewish community had little access to the male arena of party politics. Women such as Miriam Moses, who became a dynamic force in Liberal politics in London's East End during the inter-war years, were exceptions to this general rule.

However, socialist and communist traditions encouraged some women in the immigrant community to become involved in political activity in the workplace. Immigrant workers formed trade unions in order to protest at poor pay and working conditions in the sweated industries. Jewish women were particularly vulnerable to exploitation in the sweatshops and took an active role in such campaigns.

In the inter-war years, Jewish immigrant women achieved sufficient skill and confidence to create their own women's trade union groups, particularly in the garment trades. This led to representation and leadership in general trade unionism.

Jewish women who were not members of a trade union often became involved in political action by using their power as consumers. Bread sold without the Jewish Baker's Union stamp would be boycotted and Jewish immigrant women living in the Gorbals took part in the Glasgow Rent Strike of 1915.

'Up in the morn, at the break of day,
To the Sweater's den we go;
We sweat our health and strength away,
And pale and sickly grow,
That the sweaters may dwell in mansions
fair,
And wear the costliest cloths,
While our children starve in hovels bare
Where the sunlight seldom goes.'
'Sweating Song' written by Tom
Maguire to commemorate the strike of
Jewish tailors in Leeds, 1888.

*Catalogue cover of the Sweated Industries
Exhibition, displayed in London, 1906.*

Manchester Jewish Museum.

*Sweated industries were trades which relied
on cheap manual work carried out at home
or in small workshops. Often, women
worked long hours for half the pay per
'piece' that a man could expect to receive.*

In the 1840s and 1850s, women of the Jewish upper-middle classes set up the first women's charities in London and the provinces. Most were based on the idea of middle-class women visiting the homes of the Jewish working-classes, where they addressed the specific health and educational needs of immigrant women.

Jewish women charity workers acted out of compassion and a commitment to the traditions of charity in Judaism, but they were also part of the wider programme of anglicisation. In short, they sought to cultivate the moral and cultural standards of the middle-classes amongst the immigrant working-classes.

By the late 19th century, the role played by these women visitors had been acknowledged by the main communal welfare organisations. As long as women's role in the home did not suffer in the process, the involvement of women in this area of public life was accepted by the established community.

In 1902, the first National Conference of Jewish Women led to the formation of an umbrella organisation, the Union of Jewish Women. The Union aimed to co-ordinate charity work and to promote better education and training for middle-class women to enable them to play a more public role in the life of the community.

As the anglicising role of charity became less important in the inter-war years, Jewish women charity workers pioneered such important developments in communal welfare as rest homes for mothers and babies, schools for 'delicate' children and holiday homes for children of the working-classes. A few Jewish women played a vital role in promoting controversial aspects of women's health care, such as birth control, in the immigrant community and the wider society.

'Example is the best teacher, and can we expect to show the poor the importance of punctuality, the value of strenuous effort, independence of spirit, self-respect, if we furnish an object-lesson of how lightly we prize these qualities in ourselves?'
An excerpt from Miss Hannah Hyam's speech at the Conference of Jewish Women, as reported in the 'Jewish Chronicle', 1902.

'My father died when he was 43... My mother was left to struggle through. And she was a very independent woman. She could have got lots of help... But she would have sooner that we all starved to death than that she should take anything off anybody. That was her nature.'
Dinah M., Manchester.

Opposite: Card showing children in the garden at the Jewish Fresh Air Home and School, Delamere, c1935.
Manchester Jewish Museum.
Members of the Jewish Ladies' Visiting Association in Manchester went on to extend the scope of their activities in many ways. Margaret Langdon, one of the most prominent women involved in charity work in Manchester, founded the Jewish Fresh Air Home and School in Delamere and the Lymm Holiday Home for Mothers and Babies.

ON THE STREETS

Prostitution was a major issue in the 19th century. It was of special concern to Anglo-Jewry as Victorian society saw Jewish immigrants as a potential source of prostitutes. Anti-Semitic propaganda portrayed the Jewish prostitute as a threat to the moral and physical welfare of the British nation.

The established Anglo-Jewish community feared for its reputation and the sexual purity of women that Jewish religious law valued so highly. As a result, the Jewish Association for the Protection of Girls and Women (JAPGAW) was established in 1885 on the initiative of Lady Constance Rothschild Battersea.

The Association 'rescued' immigrant women who were working as prostitutes or those it believed were at most risk of becoming involved in the trade. JAPGAW set up temporary shelters and homes where middle-class women cultivated high standards of morality and where the immigrant women received training in domestic work in preparation for future employment.

Most of the women involved in the Association did not understand that some immigrant women entered the trade as a matter of choice because of the lack of better-paid alternative work. Eventually, some women reformers recognised this fact and began to press for more charitable relief for single women.

'I will seek that which is lost, and will bring again that which is driven away, and will bind up that which is broken, and will strengthen that which is sick.'
Motto of the Jewish Association for the Protection of Girls and Women, taken from Ezekiel, chapter 34 verse 16.

'In England there is a town called Leicester
In London there is such a square
Three sisters always stand there
Who doesn't know them, who doesn't?
The eldest there sells flowers
The middle one shoelaces
The youngest, O, the youngest
She sells, O, she sells herself.'
Poem originally in Yiddish, written by Morris Rosenfeld (1862-1923).

THE RIGHT TO VOTE

From the mid 19th century, the Government introduced various reforms in education, marriage and property law which affected women. However, women's right to vote was not granted and the national campaign for suffrage began.

The confidence of middle-class Jewish women was growing as a result of their increasing involvement in public life through charitable work. In 1912, the Jewish League for Woman Suffrage (JLWS) came into being, the community's equivalent of suffrage societies set up by other religious groups. Its aim was to present the religious and moral argument for women's suffrage, as an alternative to the more political standpoint of the national societies.

One of the League's objectives was to promote the

rights of Jewish women in public worship. Encouraged by the advent of Liberal Judaism, the JLWS succeeded in winning the right to vote for women seatholders in a few individual synagogues. However, it was not until 1954 that the congregations of the United Synagogues granted voting rights.

In national terms, the Government did not award the parliamentary vote to women until after the First World War, and then only to women over 30 years old. It was only in 1928 that women were able to vote on an equal basis with men.

'The justice of the demand for Woman Suffrage should appeal most especially to the Jew, to whom the evils of disenfranchisement have been, and are still in some countries, keenly felt.'
From the First Annual Report of the Jewish League for Woman Suffrage, 1913-14.

'It is felt that every Jew and Jewess should see the necessity of joining a League which represents the principles of a belief based on those of righteousness and justice, a belief which the Jew was the first to give to the world.'
From the First Annual Report of the Jewish League for Woman Suffrage, 1913-14.

'For how shall we benefit if, instead of electing our master - as we do today - we elect his wife to govern us? That is all, actually, the property vote movement stands for. It does not dream of abolishing this wage-slave society; it does not even demand Adult Suffrage.'
Rose Witcop, anarchist and campaigner for women's rights, on the middle-class interests of the suffrage movement, 1914.

THE ZIONIST CAUSE

A belief in Zionism, the creation of a Jewish homeland, was fundamental to Jewish identity from the late 19th century. Immigrant Zionist organisations merged with Anglo-Jewish groups to create the Zionist Federation of Great Britain in 1898.

The Federation was essentially a male, middle-class enterprise and, at first, Jewish women had a minor role to play except in the field of fundraising. Gradually women pressed for a more active involvement on the basis of their experience in charitable organisations and a growing awareness of women's equality.

After the First World War, women's Zionist groups were organised into the Federation of Women Zionists under the direction of Rebecca Sieff and other leading women. In 1920, the Women's International Zionist Organisation (WIZO) was founded to aid the development of a Jewish homeland in Palestine through large-scale fundraising and publicity. The Organisation promoted programmes of education and women's welfare to support the creation of a Jewish state.

Zionism provided Jewish women, for the first time, with an opportunity to enter the arena of communal politics and the expertise necessary to command a national and international public platform.

Daughters of Zion garden party, Manchester, 1910.

The Daughters of Zion was one of the earliest women's Zionist groups. It was started in Manchester by some of the future leaders of women's Zionism in Britain, such as Vera Weizmann, the wife of Chaim Weizmann who became the first president of Israel.

In the 19th and 20th centuries, a few Jewish women gained some recognition as artists in the wider society. These included Rebecca Solomon, Lily Delissa Joseph, Orovida Pissarro, Clara Klinghoffer and Gluck (Hannah Gluckstein). Most of these women came from artistic backgrounds and were supported by their families in their careers. However, it was often the personalities of these women, and not their artistic achievements themselves, which won them their notoriety.

Grace Aguilar was one of the prominent women authors in early Anglo-Jewish writing. Her works, like other Jewish books of the period, portrayed Jews of the established community as ideal Victorian and middle-class citizens. In this way she contributed to the campaign for the political emancipation of Jews in Britain. She also wrote explanations of the Jewish faith and other texts which promoted the role of women in Judaism.

Later authors, such as Amy Levy and Julia Frankau, faced criticism for their deliberately non-favourable depictions of the established community, designed to oppose the images in books such as Aguilar's. In the 20th century, Ruth Adler and Maisie Mosco became part of the growing body of Jewish authors who chose to write about the experiences of their immigrant forbears and their adjustment to life in Britain.

In the world of popular entertainment, the immigrant community brought its own cultural traditions to Britain. One of the most important of these was the Yiddish Theatre. Initially, men had played the female characters in Yiddish plays, but by the late 19th century there was a growing number of Jewish actresses. Some achieved a great deal of success in Britain and joined non-Jewish theatrical companies. However, a few immigrant women made their names directly through the British tradition of music hall entertainment.

'A preface is scarcely the place to speak of the important influence of women: yet to them, and them only, are the earliest years of man committed; from their lips must the first ideas on all subjects be received; and on them yet more particularly devolves the task of infusing that all-important but too often neglected branch of education, religion.'
Grace Aguilar in 'The Women of Israel', 1845.

'"Blessed art Thou, O Lord my God, who hast not made me a woman". No prayer goes up from the synagogue with greater fervour than this.This fact notwithstanding, it must be acknowledged that, save in the one matter of religious observance, Montague Cohen was led by the nose by his wife, whose intelligence and vitality far exceeded his own.'
Amy Levy in 'Reuben Sachs', 1888.

Bessie Cohen, London, c1905. Manchester Jewish Museum. Bessie Cohen joined the Tiller Girl dance troupe in Manchester in the 1890s when she was only 12 years old. This began her long and successful career on the English music hall stage.

THE SECOND WORLD WAR

By the 1930s, the immigrant community was losing the cultural traditions of Eastern European Jewry as the memory of the 'shtetls' faded and the children of the immigrants grew up under the influence of anglicisation. The Second World War brought the Anglo-Jewish and immigrant communities even closer together through their shared experiences of war, anti-Semitism and the refugee crisis.

From 1933 to 1939, some 50,000 refugees from Nazism fled to Britain from increasingly vicious anti-Semitic oppression in Nazi-occupied Europe. Jewish charitable organisations re-directed their efforts to provide relief and shelter for refugees, many of them children. One outcome was the League of Jewish Women, formed in 1943 to bring cohesion to the efforts of Jewish voluntary workers and to recognise the role they were playing during the war.

The British Government required that refugees seeking to enter Britain had a guaranteed means of self-support. Therefore, many Jewish young women from the Continent, often from highly educated and cultured backgrounds, sought to find work as domestics. However, once Britain entered the war, some refugee domestics were sacked by their non-Jewish employers as suspicion of people from Nazi-occupied Europe grew. In addition, many refugees were sent to internment camps as part of the Government's policy to contain what it saw as potential 'enemy aliens'.

Opposite: The Birmingham Refugee Club's children's party, c 1940s. Manchester Jewish Museum.

16

Developments

New Beginnings

After the Second World War, despite the valuable work that women had undertaken in the war effort, there was a general trend in society for married women to return to the home. This was true of the Jewish community, where men and women faced the emotional impact of the Holocaust in addition to the pressure placed on families as the British economy struggled to regain its strength.

The Holocaust experience generated added support for the Zionist movement in its search for a safe haven for the Jewish people. The Women's International Zionist Organisation (WIZO) played a central role in the formation and sustenance of the new Jewish state.

Elsewhere, the continuing involvement of Jewish women in political and charitable activities became increasingly important. Women's organisations, such as the 35 Group, took the initiative in publicising the plight of Jews forbidden to leave the Soviet Union when the main communal authorities tended to treat this issue with greater caution.

Women sought further improvements in their religious, legal and marital status, and their representation and role in the community and the wider society expanded as a result of their persistence.

Although, by 1970, some developments had taken place in the position of Jewish women in the community and in religious practice, many women had grown dissatisfied with what they saw as 'token' changes in the inequality of the sexes. Many of these women joined with non-Jews in the Women's Liberation Movement to challenge the male attitudes underlying the structure of society.

However, in the late 1970s, some Jewish women grew increasingly aware of what they saw as their double oppression as women and as Jews and began to form alternative Jewish feminist organisations. Many felt that attacks on Zionism in mainstream feminist politics included anti-Semitic undertones and marginalised the experience of Jewish women.

Jewish feminism challenged the accepted views of society and of the Jewish community in particular. Feminists debated the 'patriarchal' nature of Judaism and the validity of reclaiming religious rituals for women. This led to the exploration of women's spirituality and the foundation of religious gatherings for women, such as 'Rosh Chodesh', or New Moon, groups. The search of many Jewish women for an enhanced religious status was encouraged by the appointment of the first woman rabbi to a Reform congregation in 1975.

Jewish lesbians played a key role in Jewish feminism by asserting the right to validate identities other than the 'norm' accepted by society. Recovering the history of Jewish women also played a vital part in this process. New role models came to light in the form of women who had broken out of the mould the community had shaped for them in the past.

Although lack of funds undermined the Jewish Feminist Group in the late 1980s, Jewish feminism survived to find renewed expression in Jewish socialist networks, student organisations, women's prayer and discussion groups, and in alliances formed with other oppressed groups in society. A number of feminists took jobs in Jewish social work and women's welfare, supporting women and others who fell outside of the community's welfare systems, such as battered wives and single mothers.

'We had a lot of discussion about the fact that there are all sorts of rituals and traditions which people need to give some kind of meaning to their lives and that we... ought to be redefining those and not just taking them for granted. And I think that women have an involvement in that... I do know friends, Jewish friends, who have said, "What's the point of doing anything Jewish, because it's all patriarchal... it's all male-dominated, there's no chance of changing it". And I don't completely agree with that.'
Jane B., Manchester.

'I've always felt that Jewish identity doesn't have to be geared around religion or Zionism, that there are other ways of being Jewish... I know that there are lots of people... who would make connections with socialist traditions within Jewish history... and I think that I would ally myself with that kind of tradition.'
Jane B., Manchester.

Ordination of rabbis at the West London Synagogue,
1989. Photograph by Frank Dabba Smith. The London Museum of Jewish Life.
From left to right: Rabbis Julia Neuberger, David
Hulbert, Hugo Gryn, Elizabeth Sarah, Albert
Friedlander, Danny Rich, Jonathan Magonet, Sheila
Shulman, Lionel Blue, Ronald Berry.

During the inter-war period, Jewish religious practice based on the strictest traditions of orthodoxy suffered something of an eclipse. Under the pressure of anglicisation, a majority in the community veered towards more lax standards of orthodox observance and a minority abandoned orthodoxy for Reform and Liberal congregations. The strict religious traditions of the 'shtetl' survived in such important but beleaguered bastions as the Machzikei Hadass community and numerous small Chassidic congregations.

In the post-war years, however, there has been a significant return to stricter orthodox practice, particularly in the younger Jewish generation. The arrival of a substantial number of Hungarian Jews in the late 1950s acted as a further stimulus to the development of strictly orthodox communities in cities such as London and Manchester, and contributed to a general rise in the standards of orthodox observance throughout Anglo-Jewry.

Women's role is central to this orthodox revival. In the home, women have accepted responsibility for the maintenance of the strictest standards in such matters as dietary laws, the laws of family purity, Sabbath observance and the celebration of Jewish festivals. They have sought for their children the kind of education in which Jewish orthodoxy is an integral component.

These women have no sense of their role as unequal to that of men in the community. On the contrary, they have seen their responsibility for the home and their children as complementary to the more public role of Jewish men in synagogue affairs. Nor has orthodox women's concern for observance in the home inhibited their search for public roles in the community or in society in general.

'It's a very practical religion. It's not a religion of the synagogue, in the sense that it does not only revolve around the synagogue and prayer, although prayer is extremely important in Judaism... It revolves around the home, because most of the 'mitzvahs', most of the commandments, take place in the home. Once you understand that... you can then understand how a woman who takes her Judaism seriously in no way feels inferior but recognises that Jewish life just can't continue without her.'
Deborah G., Manchester.

Styling and fitting a 'sheitel' or wig, Manchester, 1992.

Photograph by Karen Abramson. Manchester Jewish Museum.

Many, although not all, orthodox women wear a wig after marriage as an expression of modesty.

Jewish religious law states that a woman's hair should be hidden from the sight of all men other than her husband. This is one of several laws which concern the appearance of Jewish men and women.

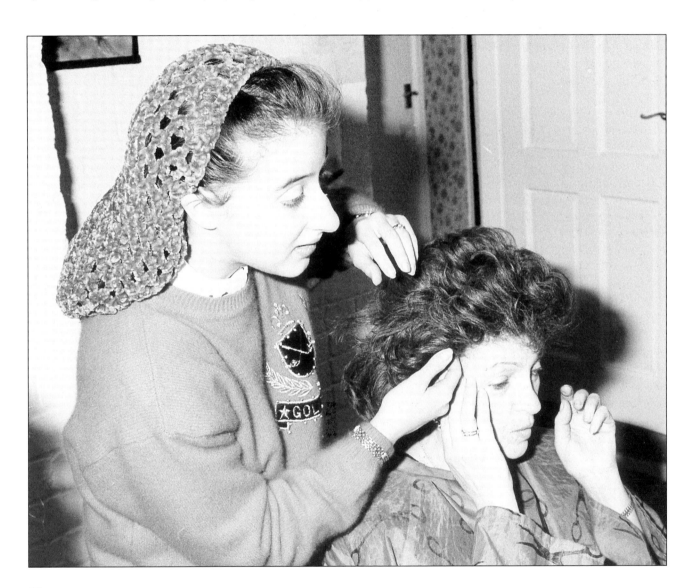

'I hate those adverts. I know that there are lots of people that find them very amusing and I do find myself giggling at them now and then, but I actually hate them. I think they do promote a stereotype that I'd rather didn't exist. I don't have a mother like that... I don't like that stereotype at all.'
Jane B., Manchester.

'Do I mind or do I like the idea of the stereotype of the Jewish woman? Now, I don't find that at all insulting because the stereotype of the Jewish woman, as I understand it at least, is that she cares enormously about her family and for her children. She is utterly devoted to them. Now, I can only see that as a very good thing, as a very positive thing... it's an indictment on modern society that it's considered to be funny that there's this woman who's worrying about her children.'
Deborah G., Manchester.

'I think that Judaism is not a barrier in any way to a Jewish woman wanting to do whatever will fulfil her. I think that the stereotype of the Jewish mother at home, only being concerned with housework and so on, it's really gone. And I think that from now on, or for the past generation really, women have been able to fulfil themselves, Jewish women, in just the same way as any non-Jewish woman... I think you can combine career and home and still run a very orthodox home. I don't think that it is any barrier at all. I think that that position has improved enormously.'
Estelle H., Manchester.

'There are dominant views in Jewish communities that sometimes marginalise people who have different experiences, and I've always felt that everybody who feels they have some call on Jewish identity has an absolute right to define that in their own way, and I think that's as true for women as it is for anyone else.'
Jane B., Manchester.

Further Reading

This is a suggested reading list for those who wish to pursue the subject of Jewish women's history further.

General and Women's Histories

Carol Adams, *'Ordinary Lives a Hundred Years Ago'*, Virago, 1982.
David Cesarani (ed.), *'The Making of Modern Anglo-Jewry'*, Basil Blackwell Ltd., 1990.
Sheila Rowbotham, *'Hidden from History'*, London, 1973.
Jerry White, *'Rothschild Buildings: Life in an East End Tenement Block. 1887-1920'*, Routledge and Kegan Paul, 1980.

Jewish Women's Histories and Women in Judaism

Rachel Biale, *'Women and Jewish Law'*, Schocken Books (USA), 1984.
Blu Greenberg, *'On Women and Judaism'*, The Jewish Publication Society of America, 1981.
Danielle Harway, Gail Chester, Val Johnson and Ros Schwartz, *'A Word in Edgeways: Jewish Feminists Respond'*, J F Publications, 1988.
Sandra Henry and Emily Taitz, *'Written Out of History: Our Jewish Foremothers'*, Biblio Press, 1983.
Susannah Heschel (ed.), *'On Being a Jewish Feminist: A Reader'*, Schocken Books (USA), 1983.
Jewish Women in London Group, *'Generations of Memories: Voices of Jewish Women'*, The Women's Press, 1989.
Elizabeth Koltun (ed.), *'The Jewish Woman'*, Schocken Books (USA), 1976.
Linda Gordon Kuzmack, *'Woman's Cause: The Jewish Women's Movement in England and the United States'*, Ohio State University Press, 1990.
Sydney Stahl Weinberg, *'The World of Our Mothers: The Lives of Jewish Immigrant Women'*, Schocken Books (USA), 1988.

Articles by Rickie Burman, Rosalyn Livshin, Tony Kushner and Lara Marks.